NASTY PEOPLE

JAY CARTER

CONTEMPORARY
BOOKS

CHICAGO · NEW YORK

Library of Congress Cataloging-in-Publication Data

Nasty people : how to stop being hurt by them without
becoming one of them / Jay Carter.
    p.   cm.
Bibliography: p.
ISBN 0-8092-4406-3
1. Criticism, Personal.   I. Title.
BF637.C74C37   1989
158'.2—dc19   88-34263
                                                              CIP

Some of the material herein was originally published in a
slightly different form in the author's book, *Self-Analysis*,
© 1979 by James J. Carter.

Published by Contemporary Books, Inc.
180 North Michigan Avenue, Chicago, Illinois 60601
Manufactured in the United States of America
International Standard Book Number: 0-8092-4406-3

Published simultaneously in Canada by Beaverbooks, Ltd.
195 Allstate Parkway, Valleywood Business Park
Markham, Ontario L3R 4T8 Canada

Dedicated to our great-great-grandchildren

Acknowledgments

Many thanks to the following people for their help with the book: Linda Aglow, Dr. Astrid Jimenez Alvarado, Sandra DiSantis, Stanley Dudkin, Lotis Gudez, Dr. Monica P. Hottenstein, Dr. Sanford Mintz, Art Parker, Dr. Orest M. Pawluk, Stacy Prince, Jan Radabaugh, Sheila Sen-Carter, Barbara Stender, Dr. Margaret Verhulst, Nickie Williams, Anne Marie Zagnojny, and all my students. A special thanks to Dave Leiter for his encouragement.

Contents

From a Student

I first met Jay Carter through his "Communications Workshop" course at a local adult evening school. I signed up for the course to help in my never-ending search for better-spoken expression. The course helped my speaking, but it was really about something else. It was about people, and how they think and act. In other words, it was a course in practical psychology.

As part of this course, Jay taught us about *invalidation*. Invalidation is what I used to call "putting other people down to bring yourself up." But even though I had discovered the phenomenon of invalidation on my own, I didn't know where it came from, why it existed, how it really worked, or what to call it. Most of all, I had no idea how deadly it could be to life, liberty, and the pursuit of happiness.

What I learned in Jay Carter's class about invalidation has changed my life. Now, at the very least, when invalidation is used in my presence, I know it instantly—whether it comes from someone else or from me (blush). I do my best to educate those involved about the "mechanics" of invalidation. To do this, I passed out copies of Jay's paper on invalidation.

1

After a while, though, copying and distributing those pages got to be a lot of work. Besides, at that rate, only about one person in ten million will ever learn what invalidation is all about. It's too important to keep it a secret.

So I've nagged, bullied, and generally pestered Jay into writing this little book on invalidation. I think you'll be glad I did.

L. David Leiter

From the Author

Dear Reader,

Every book has a story behind it, and I thought you might like to know this one. My motivation to gather this information came from my own situation. I felt unhappy and didn't know why. I felt as if I were stuck in some sort of trap that I couldn't identify.

While I was pursuing my graduate degree in psychology, I kept a journal in which I wrote about my personal experiences, meetings with clients and professionals, and course readings. After a while, I began to notice that some of the "dysfunctional" personalities I was reading about were evident in people I knew. Then one day, while I was away on business and out of my daily environment, it hit me. I realized, objectively, that I was being invalidated. Constantly.

When I first acknowledged how much I had been invalidated, I was enraged. It took me months to work off this anger. I wrote a lot of negative things about invalidators. I ran hard and fast. I purchased a punching bag. I chopped wood with a vengeance. I screamed obscenities when I was alone in my car. I passed my writings around to people so they could help me agree

3

what terrible, no-good people invalidators are. I hated invalidators. I was out to *get* them.

Then, one day, I shared my writings with a good friend at work. I had always admired this man.

He came back to me with tears in his eyes saying, "I am an invalidator. I have been making my mother miserable for years."

I was taken aback! I didn't want to believe him. He asked me, "How can I stop?" I stumbled over myself. I had nothing to tell him. My whole agenda had been to *attack* invalidators, not to help them. Driving home that evening, I realized that I had become an invalidator. I thought of my friend and his plight, and I cried. How could I have been so unaware?

I began looking for answers. I was serious now, and less enraged. I began throwing myself in front of invalidators just to see what happened. (You know what happens when you lie on railroad tracks? Right. A train passes over your body.) I studied mothers and fathers of invalidators. I studied criminals. I studied double-bind theory and every book I could get my hands on.

Finally I began to see the whole cycle. I began to understand the importance of "the truth, the whole truth, and nothing but the truth."

Once I understood everything, my self-esteem returned. I was able to handle people better. Instead of spitting and hissing at invalidation, I could handle it with humor or by being confrontational and direct. I was no longer terribly affected by invalidation. Instead of feeling outraged, I would just feel a little nudge. Instead of attacking invalidation like a Rambo, I would merely put it out with the rest of the garbage.

Once I discovered the secret to my own happiness, I began sharing my new understanding with others, and I saw it make a real difference in their lives. I witnessed miracles when I taught adult school classes on human awareness.

At first, I presented students with *my* solutions to invalidating behavior. As time went on, however, I found it worked much better in the long run if I just presented the problem and allowed people to come up with their own solutions. It seems that we each make our own set of keys to life. We make each notch in each key from our experiences and the advice of others, sometimes through sheer luck or the grace of God. These keys unlock the secrets of life for us. Every once in a while, someone stumbles on a master key—a key that helps others create their keys more easily. I am sure I am not the only one who discovered the master key outlined in this book. In some ways, in fact, anyone could have written it.

About the time people started bugging me to write a book, I'd begun to realize that I *had* to write it. I needed to reach as many people as possible with my exciting discoveries.

Most teachers will tell you that teachers learn as much from their students as students do from their teachers. I know that when I'm teaching, I always "find" an answer to a question, even if I didn't know that answer to that question before. I often find myself saying, "So *that's* it!" after responding to a new question. I had much the same experience when writing *Nasty People*. In the midst of writing drudgery . . . *bam!* The cause of poor self-esteem was sitting there staring at me. The *major* cause. Perhaps the *only* cause. It seems I had found another key, the key to self-esteem.

What you are paying for in this book is data. I have worked very hard, with the assistance of many people, to present these data to you in a simple and concise way. I don't care for books that force me to run through 125 to 500 pages just for an idea that could have been presented in 5. I've tried to spare you that.

How do I know these ideas are on target? Because people have told me they are. I have presented my work to thousands of people in colleges (such as Temple University), industry (companies such as IBM), and various adult education programs.

The concepts in this book may not make you happy. But they may make things clear enough so that you can stop being *unhappy*. I'll leave it up to you to do what you need to do to make yourself happy. For a start, let's get the monkey (whoever he, she, or it is) off your back.

I mentioned earlier that I *had* to write this book. For what good would my "master key" do my great-great-grandchild if invalidation is still running rampant? Did you know that the average person has 512 great-great-great-great-great-grandchildren? Here's to them!

Jay Carter
January 1989

It has been my experience that some people will have a strong reaction to the knowledge in this book. My heart goes out to them. Those who have been victims of invalidation may become enraged. Those who have recognized themselves as invalidators may become sad or remorseful. Trust your feelings. If you feel sad . . . cry. If you feel angry . . . get mad. Don't hold it in. Let it out. But remember these are *your* feelings. Don't dump responsibility for your own feelings on anyone else. Blaming other people will not help . . . even if they *are* to blame.

Overview

This book is about that sector of the population that contributes to a specific phenomenon called *invalidation*. Invalidation could very well be the major cause of poor self-esteem, mental anguish, and overall unhappiness. With this in mind, you can see that this book may contain some of the most important information you've ever read and may significantly change your life.

Invalidation is propagated in our society by all of us. Only 1 percent intentionally spread this misery to manipulate and control others. Twenty percent do it semiconsciously as a defense mechanism. The rest of us do it only occasionally, usually unconsciously and unintentionally. Invalidation can be found to greater and lesser degrees in various societies. Happier individuals develop in societies in which invalidation is at a minimum.

Invalidation is a general term that I use in this book to describe one person injuring or trying to injure another. An invalidation can range anywhere from a shot in the back to a "tsk, tsk." A rolling of the eyeballs can be an invalidation, and so can a punch in the nose. It is usually the sneaky mental invalidations that cause the most damage. A punch in the nose is obvious, and it

9

heals. However, an attack on self-esteem—at the right moment and in the right way—can last a lifetime. Destroying a person's capability to be happy for a whole lifetime is probably worse than any physical damage one person can do to another. The major reason invalidation occurs so often is that it *works* (in the short run). The sneaky invalidation works because a punch in the nose is obvious and can be returned to the insulting party, but the mental attack may go unnoticed and unpunished while it injures and manipulates its victim.

What if the process of invalidation were exposed?

Long ago, germs were unseen and unknown, yet they wreaked havoc. When Pasteur detected all these little bugs running around the body, people got upset. They put Pasteur away. Nobody wanted to think of little bugs that you couldn't see crawling all over you and inside you. Today, thanks to Pasteur and others, germs are known about and combated.

By the same token, forming a lynch mob to hang invalidators will not solve anything.

Curing underhanded invalidation might not be easy, but it is much easier than dealing with germs; we won't have to invent antitoxins or penicillin. The big part of the cure for invalidation is achieved when we simply spot it. Remaining undetected and unchallenged is what gives invalidation its power.

Nevertheless, the people who get invalidated *allow* themselves to be invalidated, and they are just as responsible as the people doing it are. It is every person's duty to learn to recognize and divert or defuse the devaluating attack.

If invalidation didn't work . . . nobody would do it.

Psychology books contain theories. This one is no different. The only thing that separates useful theories from useless theories is practical applicability. Pasteur's theory about germs would still be in some book or other and Pasteur would be an obscure historical figure if his ideas had not been used to revolutionize medical practice. The best, most interesting theory is worthless if nothing changes when you *use* it.

"The small Hitlers are around us every day."
—Robert Payne

1
The Invalidator

INTRODUCING THE INVALIDATOR

It's hard to recognize an invalidator, because a truly good one can bypass the scrutiny of your logical mind, and you find yourself feeling bad without knowing why. The invalidator is underhanded, and the person being invalidated is often unsuspecting except for knowing that he or she feels bad. The invalidator actually feels inferior to some other person, so he or she tries to make that other person feel small. Thus, the invalidator can control the victim. Have you met anyone like this? Whether you are completely aware of it or not, you probably have. You probably know one, or several, invalidators.

The invalidator uses various suppressive mechanisms to chop away at your self-esteem. He pretends to acknowledge something you are proud of, then later makes some negative insinuation about it. He feels out what you think your shortcomings are and then exploits them at calculated times when he knows you are vulnerable. The invalidator may persist in invalidating you until you succumb. He *has to* control you because he perceives you as being superior to him. He takes accusations that

have "some truth," and fires them at you "in all hon-
esty," "just being your friend," "to help you."

The difference between an invalidator and a real
friend is that a real friend will tell you one negative
thing about yourself and then back off to give you space
to consider it. An invalidator will lay many of your faults
out for you and persist until you feel as big as the period
at the end of this sentence. An invalidator will pick out
the qualities about yourself that are most important to
you and then tear them apart. An invalidator will listen
to you share something that you don't like about yourself and then later use it against you. This is all done in
such a subtle way that you are unaware of it.

If you do confront an invalidator on what she is
doing, she will say something like, "Oh, come on now!
I love you. I'm your friend. Where did you get these silly
ideas?" And she may *really* like you. She may *really* want
to be your friend . . . but only on her terms and only after
she has you in her control. She will make you look silly
for even thinking such things about her. She may make
you feel guilty or cheap in front of your friends for
accusing her of invalidating you. She may get angry at
you for your accusations. Whatever she can do to invalidate you further, she will. If she really thinks you are
onto her, she may apologize and then not invalidate you
again . . . until later when you are unsuspecting.

In short, the invalidator does whatever is necessary to
control you. He is control-crazy, and any time he perceives himself to be not in control, he will be scared.

PORTRAIT OF AN INVALIDATOR

One of the most famous invalidators was Adolph Hitler.
He was quite typical of the controlling invalidator. He
was a brilliant man. He created beautiful pictures. He
was a writer. He saved the lives of his comrades when he
was in the regular army. He loved his dogs. He had a

love relationship with Eva Braun. He spoke beautiful words, for example:

> Since 1914 when, as a volunteer, I made my modest contribution in the World War which was forced upon the Reich, over thirty years have passed.
>
> In these three decades only love for my people and loyalty to my people have guided me in all my thoughts, actions, and life. They gave me the strength to make the most difficult decisions, such as no mortal has yet had to face. I have exhausted my time, my working energy, and my health in these three decades.
>
> It is untrue that I or anybody else in Germany wanted war in 1939.

Not only was he eloquent, but he lived up to his promises. He brought Germany out of a recession, making his words credible. People believed in him. He was never to blame. He was *righteous*.

He never killed anyone face to face, but got his followers to do it. The sight of the Jews being slaughtered sickened him. He barely looked, the *one* time he witnessed it. He *really believed* in what he was doing. Before he gained power, he tried to commit suicide, but one of his friends (a superior officer) saved him from it.

If you had met Hitler, you might think he was charming. You would probably not guess what devastation he was capable of. The following are excerpts from *The Life and Death of Adolf Hitler* by Robert Payne (italics are my own):

> Hitler was the arch-destroyer, determined to stamp out and destroy everything in the world *that did not serve his purposes*.
>
> Yet the man who spilled so much blood, and was

so bloodless, never dared to look at the dead or the
dying, never visited a military hospital, and *never
showed any sympathy* for the maimed, the wounded,
the blind. He drove millions of people insane and
millions died in his concentration camps. He had
no conception of the suffering he had brought to
the world; and had he known, it would have made
no difference. When he traveled through bombed
towns, he drew the window shades for fear that the
sight of the destruction he had caused would
weaken his resolution. In darkness, behind shut-
tered windows, remote from the world as in a grave
he terrorized *the world he never understood* and
never wanted to understand.

He especially liked one portrait of himself with
his eyes raised to heaven in angelic innocence. He
also admired a portrait of himself in shining ar-
mor.

The voice is seductive, and his *logic*, if his prem-
ises are accepted, *is unimpeachable.*

He *believes* in his own absolute authority over
the people.

In the present age we are only too aware of his
existence, for he still walks among us.

It is strange that we do not speak about Hitlers
in the plural. . . . The small Hitlers are around us
every day, tormenting us with their promises, re-
joicing in our weaknesses, demanding our trust,
our votes, and our lives, while remaining totally
indifferent to everything except their thirst for
power. Power to *order the lives of other men consoles
them for their own insufficiencies,* their lack of
humanity. They *must* have power or perish, and it
is all one to them if they misuse their power or
crush others in their efforts to seize power.

So you see, these invalidators can be particularly nasty characters if they get into positions of power. And they are always, in fact, striving for positions of power because they are "small Hitlers" with an obsessive need to control people and events.

The more clever invalidators don't use their powers until it's absolutely necessary. The invalidator can appear to be quite friendly for a very long time. Then when it comes time for a promotion in management, and it's either you or him, he chews you up and spits you out in front of your upper management before you know what hit you—all the while, of course, being your good buddy. He will even invent perfectly logical reasons why you wouldn't have wanted the job anyway. That is, unless he wants to destroy you completely. Then he will just make you look bad in front of everyone for a long time. He might do all this with information you told him about yourself in confidence, when he so endearingly listened to you.

You've probably met many people capable of invalidation, but it probably caught you off guard and perhaps you didn't understand how it worked. The next section of this book will explain the methods used by invalidators. Read it thoroughly, but keep in mind that there are many methods of invalidation and many ways to handle an invalidator. And the minute you handle an invalidation is the minute it starts looking for another outlet.

There are no "cookbooks" for handling invalidation. That's why this book is so small. You need to know the essence or nature of invalidation so you can handle it *your* way. Toward the end of the book, I'll give you a few examples of how it can be handled, but once you *see* invalidation, you must find how you deal with it best. You need to develop a strategy that fits your own personality and ethics.

METHODS OF THE INVALIDATOR
UNCERTAINTY

One method of an invalidator is to keep you in a constant state of uncertainty. She rarely gives you an answer. Just vagueness—no commitment. She makes you feel unsure of your environment for long periods of time, until your adaptive ability begins to fail. The invalidator may do this in any number of ways.

For example, the invalidator will suddenly become understanding, lovable, and very nice to you. Things will remain this way until you become trusting. Then with one swift blow, he makes you uncertain again by means of criticism, insinuations, or suppressed rage. You may ask, "What happened? We were doing so well." The invalidator answers, "What do you mean 'what happened?' Is something wrong?"

"Well, yes. You are not the same," you say. The reply is: "What?!" (fire eyes turn on). "Really! You are driving me crazy! I can never be sure what you are going to come up with next." Then sarcastically and mockingly: "What happened? We were doing so well!"

And there you are in a state of uncertainty. Again caught up in the projections of your favorite invalidator. And you say to yourself, "Gee, I guess he really wasn't aware . . . or maybe it's me . . . maybe I'm reading into things too much. Maybe I'm going crazy."

And just about that time, your invalidator looks at you oh, so very lovingly and so concerned, and says, "Oh, honey, maybe you should see a doctor, you just aren't acting like yourself." He runs his fingers through your hair with the utmost look of concern and says, "I wouldn't want anything to happen to my baby." A slight tear forms in the corner of his eye. "Go see Dr. Schmidt tomorrow, honey, and tell him about the problems you've been having." Then he quickly turns, sits back down on the couch, and reads the paper.

And then there are the times you think, "Maybe he's changed. He just bought me a new car and told me he loved me. He's been telling me how wonderful I am for a week/month." Things are great for a while. Then inevitably, after you trust him again, he begins all over again with the criticisms, the insinuations, the anger. He has you trapped in a sickening feeling of uncertainty.

PROJECTION

Projection is a psychological maneuver that can be explained rather simply. It is a favorite tool of the invalidator: she simply takes her own feelings and puts the responsibility for them onto another person, as if these feelings originate with the other person.

For example, a person who doesn't like you says, "I don't think you like me." This statement perhaps gets you questioning yourself. It thereby puts the attention on you, and you start looking at your own feelings instead of noticing the other person's feelings. This provides a good hiding place for the other person. The one doing the accusing is often calling you to task for things she herself is doing.

Isn't it ironic that the one who lashes out at others for their negative feelings or misdeeds is often guilty of the same failings in thought, word, or deed? When someone attacks you for something you didn't do, it says more about her than it does you.

For example, if I were a dedicated husband, and my wife started accusing me of cheating on her, I would know almost for sure that she had done it in thought, word, or deed. You can tell an enormous amount about people by their projections. Listen closely.

GENERALIZATION

Watch out for generalizations. An invalidator will often use generalizations, which are simply exaggerations of small truths. The more truth there is in a generalization, the more it can be exaggerated.

For example, when you get home from work, your spouse might greet you with, "You are inconsiderate." (Translation: You forgot to bring home the milk.) "You are irresponsible." (You forgot to bring home the milk.) "You are stupid." (You forgot to bring home the milk.)

Your self-esteem is attacked instead of the problem. The problem is "There's no milk." The problem is not that you are inconsiderate, irresponsible, or stupid.

Even if you were stupid, what could you possibly do about it? How can you attack the problem of being stupid? (Probably if you went back to the store to get the milk, your IQ would increase by leaps and bounds!) A person who uses generalizations like this does so to be in control of another.

JUDGMENT

The preceding example contains another of the invalidator's methods: judgments. The person who says, "You are irresponsible" has assumed another hidden statement to back it up. That assumption is "Everyone would agree that you are irresponsible. Obviously so."

And then, since you also might agree that forgetting the milk was irresponsible, you might assume that perhaps you *are* irresponsible. You begin to question and doubt yourself, especially if your inadequacies are pointed out frequently.

A person who is really responsible for his or her feelings would say, "I am angry that you didn't bring home the milk." But the invalidator projects the responsibility for this judgment onto the world, as if *everyone* would agree that you are no good. In doing this, the invalidator attacks your self-esteem instead of the real problem.

This is a simple explanation, but perhaps you can think of times when a generalization or judgment really had you going. Especially if the judgment about you was made by someone you love or respect. You were upset by this judgment even if you don't think of yourself as stupid, or irresponsible, or whatever title the invalidator was attaching to you. After all, you don't want him thinking that of you, so you are motivated to impress him, to please him, to get him to remove the unpleasant titles he's giving you. All the while, of course, he is in control of the situation.

MANIPULATION

Manipulation is *bad* control. There is such a thing as *good* control. Good control is ethical and includes a fair exchange, "please," and "thank you." The invalidator wants to control . . . period. If good control fails, she uses bad control. If the usual methods fail, she uses devious, covert, or overt methods, because she is *compelled* to win or to be in control. You may often be pressured to let her have things her way. She will use sneaky methods of manipulation, or outright methods of domination. An invalidator, by definition, is a manipulator.

SNEAK ATTACK

"I don't want to upset you but. . . ." (He probably *does* want to upset you.) "I don't mean to interrupt . . " (Right!!) "I don't mean to rain on your parade." (Uh huh.) "Don't let this bother you, but . . . ." (Bother. Bother.) "I hope this doesn't insult you, but . . . ." (Here comes an insult!) His voice will be soft. His face will show concern. His words are sweet, but underneath are daggers. The tongue is a mighty weapon, a sharp sword.

DOUBLE MESSAGE

The invalidator says to you, "How are you?" But he verbalizes the word *you* in something of a guttural tone—the voice of disgust.

If you respond with "Screw you, Jack!" then Jack will very innocently relate to everyone that you must be in a bad mood because all he did was ask how you were, and you told him off. Jack will never come right out and say it, but he insinuates that you are a real son of a bitch . . . all the while making excuses for you (such magnanimity!).

It is well known that double messages in childhood contribute to schizophrenia. The mother who says, "I love you," and then goes rigid when her child hugs her is sending a very destructive double message.

You will find many double messages like this from an invalidator. But they may not be so obvious. Usually, you end up feeling weird or bad without realizing why.

For example, your friendly neighborhood invalidator might find out that your grandmother died and proceed to tell you stories about inheritance feuds. "You know, it's a shame sometimes when brothers and sisters go through estates and never speak to each other again." Then the invalidator will give you the facts (actually generalizations) about others he knows who have had family splits over inherited money. He will do this especially if he has a hint that you don't get along so well with one of your siblings. He is pretending to send messages of concern and love, but in truth he is throwing psychological daggers.

CUTTING COMMUNICATION

Another valuable verbal tool for an invalidator is cutting communication. She asks you a question about yourself, then cuts you off before you finish answering.

Or she asks you a leading question like, "Do you still quarrel with your wife?" You can't answer this question without appearing wrong. She walks out in the middle of a conversation, creating a logjam of unspoken thoughts piled up in your mind.

"BUILDING YOU *UP*, CUTTING YOU *DOWN*"

Be careful who you depend on for your self-esteem. If you depend on others, the invalidator will shower you with compliments until you are totally dependent on him, then he will take you apart piece by piece until you are in his control.

The whole idea is to get you introverted and introspective so that you don't notice what is going on outside yourself. Once you start looking anxiously and self-consciously at yourself, the invalidator will subtly draw your attention to all your most negative qualities. This will make you feel weaker, more susceptible to control.

By doing this, the invalidator can pull you down to size. He may feel that he worries too much, while you usually appear calm and confident. If he can get you to come down to his level and start worrying more, then he feels superior. And oh, by the way, he will be the first to offer to help.

After a while, you worry only about what *he* thinks. What *he* will do. Whether *he* will be angry at you or not. You stop looking at yourself after a while because you see so much wrong with you that you totally depend on *him* for your sense of worth.

And then when even *he* doesn't want you . . . ?

THE DOUBLE BIND

One of the meanest, sneakiest tricks of invalidators is the double bind. Logic will not solve this problem. Only *awareness* will solve it. The invalidator puts you in a position where you are "wrong if you do, wrong if you don't."

This can be best demonstrated by an ancient lesson. Let's suppose you are a student of an ancient Oriental institution of learning.

You show up at the master's house for your daily lesson. The master invites you in, and both of you sit down for a cup of tea. Just as you are ready to pick up your cup of tea, the master pulls out a large stick from under the table and says, "This is your lesson for today. If you pick up the cup of tea, I will hit you with this stick. And if you don't pick up the cup of tea, I will hit you with this stick."

I have presented this problem to thousands of people in my classes. Ninety-five percent of them have been so caught up in the logic of the problem and the *thinking* of a solution that they could not solve it. A typical answer is "Well, I would drink the tea. As long as I'm going to get hit anyway, I may as well enjoy it." Other people say, "I would slap the master in the face and get one in before he hits me."

There are two answers that will *solve* the problem. One is a good answer because it solves the problem while still maintaining a relationship with the master. The answer is to *take the stick away*. Think about it.

The other answer is to *walk away*. This answer solves the problem but cuts off further interaction with the master.

The whole beginning to the solution is to get out of the introverting logic set up by the invalidator so you can view the *whole* situation. The whole situation involves you, the master, the logic, the game . . . the situation.

For example, right now, you are reading the words on this page. Your logical mind is right now interpreting these words and making sense of them. You could very well be introverted into this reading. You may not be aware of the whole environment you are in—the colors and sounds around you. We assume sometimes that when we read, we must concentrate on the reading so much that we cut off our other perceptions and only *think*. This is not necessary. You *can* read these words and still be aware of what's going on around you—what your feelings are, your body position, who or what is around you, and so on.

There is a certain feeling that goes along with a double bind, a feeling of being trapped. This feeling should be your cue to start being aware of your environment. That feeling should automatically make you stop thinking, stop introverting. Remove yourself from the immediate situation, and take a *look* at what's happening. Once an invalidator has you introverted and thinking, you are under his or her control.

The solution: *Do not introvert.* Do not defend yourself. Try to notice what makes the invalidator want to put you on the spot.

Let's take a recent local example of a double-bind situation.

A woman attending my classes was very excited about the work we were doing, feeling that she was getting a lot out of it. Her behavior was changing. She was re-gaining her confidence and becoming more self-assured.

Her husband was threatened by this and felt rather out of control. He gave her this ultimatum.

"It's either that damn class or our marriage." Logi-cally, of course, the choice is easy. No one is going to give up a marriage just for the sake of attending a class. How would that look to everyone? "I gave up my mar-riage to attend Jay Carter's class."

If her husband had constantly been threatening her this way, it might not have had such force. But he saved up this extreme type of threat, and only called it on special occasions when he needed a large portion of control.

The wife popped out of her introversion and took a look at the game. She saw the typical elements of con-trol.

1. It was *his* game.
2. It had the threat of a disastrous effect on her.
3. The outcome was all up to her. She was totally re-sponsible for her reaction to his threat.

Here is the way she handled it with him: "I am not going to choose (i.e., I'm not going to play your game). I am going to attend class, and *you* can choose . . . our marriage or this class."

She used a technique I call "mirroring." She threw the invalidator's game right back into his lap. When you give him the responsibility for his actions, an invalida-tor will almost always back down. All those threats he throws around don't just roll off the victim's back—they *bounce*, right back to him. If his victims use this tech-nique frequently enough, an invalidator will eventually stop using his little tricks. Let's face it. If every time you

kicked a dog, it bit you, you would think twice before you kicked.

You may be wondering what happened to the guy and his wife. Well, they are fine. The more respect for herself she gained, the more respect *he* had for her. He stopped using invalidation on her when it stopped working. They went through a bad time for a while when she let out all of her pent-up anger on him. The tables reversed for a time with her as the invalidator and him as the victim. The invalidation eventually ran itself out, and the affinity bloomed again. They learned to get angry at one another in a more workable fashion.

It may not work out as well for everyone. Some people have built up resentment for so long that they cannot continue a relationship any longer. The relationship may have died long since, with only the control mechanisms still in place.

If there is any chance at all of reviving a relationship, I highly recommend it. People who are capable of being rotten are usually equally capable of being wonderful. I've seen people who use the mechanism of invalidation make 180-degree turns in attitude. I don't quite understand it because I myself change slowly. Nevertheless, once an invalidator learns to handle his anger and stops invalidating, he can make a sudden change and never do it again.

The understanding and willingness to *do* something

about it are key factors. But beware of sudden changes that merely lead to further manipulation. If your beloved invalidator says he understands now what he's been doing and vows to reform, but then is unwilling to discuss it again, don't trust him.

INVALIDATOR: AN ARCHETYPE

Do you remember a friend that you imitated? Do you act like your mother sometimes? Your father? It could be said that you entered into the "archetype" of your mother, father, or friend for that time you acted like them. An archetype was designated by Carl Jung as a complete personality type, one that recurs throughout human experience. Common archetypes are those of the warrior, the hunter, or the demon.

You probably have several personalities that you have developed yourself. Your "mom" or "dad" role. Your "professional" image. Your "kid" personality. These are separate types that you develop and use every day. It's almost like having separate suits of clothing for different occasions in the closet of your mind. If you are a woman with children, you probably have your own "mom" personality. This might be made up of:

- Your own ideas about what a mom should do, act, and say
- Behaviors borrowed from your mom (including those things that you said you would never do to your kids . . . but find yourself doing anyway)
- Behaviors borrowed from television moms, other people's moms, your grandmother, etc.

So what am I getting at here, anyway?

OK. Let me paint a personality for you. Did you ever notice that most invalidators are not that way all the time? That's what makes them so difficult to understand sometimes. They are unpredictable! You never know what might set them off. (Sometimes you *do* know.)

All of a sudden, it's like a demon takes them over. This nice person becomes a ranting maniac, or else he becomes a very withdrawn, biting person. Or else he seems nice, but you suddenly feel bad around him without knowing why. There are various degrees of obviousness when invalidation occurs. And there is a psychological cycle that happens to each invalidator when invalidating behavior appears.

What follows are the three degrees of invalidating behavior from the most obvious to the most covert.

MOST OBVIOUS PERSONALITY

This person appears to have no conscience at all and sometimes seems crazed enough to be capable of *anything*. He seems about to lose control at any second. He exudes and reeks of anger, outrage, and righteousness. He threatens to do things that are the most liable to do you in. He may sometimes threaten to do outlandish things while smiling at you as if enjoying your plight or he makes it appear that you deserve his disapproval, that you have surely done something to set him off. At other times he is overly loving and apologetic.

Sometimes too much liquor can turn on this demonic personality in a person.

LESS OBVIOUS PERSONALITY

She points out your weaknesses. She reminds you of your past misdoings. She tries to get your agreement that things you do are wrong, and is constantly proving how bad you are. She acts as if the good things you do aren't that great, or "you finally did something good *for a change*." She is righteous. When you point out to this person some wrongdoing of *hers*, she will bombard you with all of *your* wrongdoings, in an indignant manner. Her memory for recalling your mistakes is usually fantastic. Later, she may get upset: "How could you say that about me? You hurt me." She proves to you what an ass you are. She is jealous of your possessions and envies your accomplishments. She belittles you in groups.

LEAST OBVIOUS

This person appears to be your good buddy. He always has some negative thing to tell you in "good faith." He loves to be "honest" and "truthful." He gossips about you behind your back and is secretly jealous of you. He tells you secrets about the negative things other people are thinking of you. He pays you compliments that are really double messages, insinuat-ing that you are paranoid if you confront him on his double messages. It's possible he has a higher opinion of you than he does of himself.

As these types indicate, nobody is an invalidator all the time. More often, a perfectly wonderful person turns from the one you love into a monster who hates you and can't think of enough ways to degrade you. Your loved one is temporarily just like a devil. This demonic form is *not all there is* in this person; it is an archetype he or she enters at times. While someone is in it, this demonic personality is complete—it has its own thoughts, ideas, ethics, and behavior. A person may enter into this behavior consciously, or may slip into it unconsciously when something in the environment triggers it.

The worst case is a Hitler who consciously goes into this personality at calculated times. In addition, a Hitler develops this archetype to perfection so that it works almost every time.

Most people slip into the invalidator archetype unconsciously, reacting to subtle and sometimes unnoticed cues in the environment. These poor people have been exposed to invalidators in the past—often a parent or sibling who just never could be pleased or approving. Unconsciously, without understanding the source of their trouble, they become invalidators at various unpredictable times. They are running on automatic pilot; they don't know what they are doing, and they don't know what else to do. Sliding into this role is no great advantage, either to the victim or the invalidator. The invalidator can win a lot of battles with the behavior, but in the long run loses the war. He or she may get to control others for a time, but after a while no one wants to be around an invalidator. Of course, some invalidators (like Hitler) are so clever and subtle that they always have others around them to control.

IDENTIFYING AN INVALIDATOR

Perhaps you have met someone who flattered you by being possessive and jealous. Then later you were puzzled when this person treated you condescendingly. This person would be interested in you especially when you had the attention of others, but then become bored with you when you devoted most of your time to him. He might become enraged when you did something against his will or against his opinion. When you demonstrated you had a mind of your own, he might become more enraged. Making love to this person would seem like more of a satisfaction of his libido than a sincere expression of love. Everyone probably has these tendencies sometimes, but the invalidator has them to a great degree.

To deal with an invalidator, first you have to be able to detect one. Methods of invalidation can be so clever, so sneaky, and so suppressive that you might not be able to see them. If you know someone that you always feel bad with, it could be your insecurities, or it could be an invalidator at work. Probably both.

Simply stated, your insecurities come from past experiences that you never really noticed or understood or accepted, that have been embedded in your subconscious and wait, ready to cause pain or defensiveness or introversion at odd moments when you least suspect they are at work. A clever invalidator finds your most sensitive spots, and plays on them to gain control over you by making you feel vulnerable.

The important thing to look for is not the various traits of an invalidator. The important thing to look at is how you feel over a certain period of time when you are in the company of a possible invalidator. It is not necessary to see all the mechanisms an invalidator uses. Somewhere you will pick up the way things are going with this person.

You should get enough data in this book to enable you to spot an invalidator. Follow what you feel you know. If you feel constant jabs of discomfort when you are with someone, take a look at what he or she is doing.

This book has not even begun to describe all the techniques of invalidation; there are a lot more tricks and traits to which a much longer book could be devoted. However, this book is not just about "things to watch for in others." Reading about the invalidator is not intended to make you paranoid. Don't read this information and become a recluse. Just notice that these forms of behavior exist in some people at some times, and be prepared to handle them when they do. These traits are for you to know about *so that you don't introvert on yourself.*

I estimate that approximately 1 percent of the population is made up of bona fide conscious invalidators. Twenty percent of the population are "semiconscious" invalidators. If you are reading this book, the chances are excellent that you are not the 1 percent mentioned. That kind of person would not want to attempt the self-improvement contained in this book.

While reading this book, you may notice yourself having intense feelings. Just keep plodding on through. You may need some time alone after reading parts of this book so you can reintegrate yourself. Allow your emotions to arise. Trust your feelings.

True invalidators are not easy to spot. But if you pay attention to your feelings, and to people who are connected to invalidators, you will be able to recognize them. You will notice that people who are connected to invalidators are not in the best condition, while the invalidator seems just fine. The invalidator's family may seem to be all "mental cases" while he or she is the only sane one. It is actually just the opposite.

"No one can make you feel inferior without your consent."

—Eleanor Roosevelt

2
The Victim

With all due respect, if you choose to be connected to a true member of the nasty 1 percent, a bona fide conscious invalidator, because you think you can handle it, there are some things you should know. He *has* to control. It's survival for him—ego survival. If he sees himself as lesser than you, there will always be the push to reduce you so he can control you. The very first time you are sick or run-down or in trouble, or in any way down, he will try to make sure you *stay* down. If you want to hang around playing that sort of game, it's your business. Your invalidator may be very charming and adventurous and probably very intelligent. If your invalidator "turns you on," have fun while it lasts. Misery is around the next corner. You may think you'll never be in that vulnerable position of feeling "down." But by staying connected to a "one-percenter," you are creating it. So Bon Voyage. . . .

Allowing yourself to be under the constant stress of always having to react to an invalidator could lead to psychosomatic illness. I have known several people who were connected to invalidators by marriage or family. Some of these victims had ulcers, heart disease, cancer, and other disorders. Being under the daily stress of dealing with an invalidator does eat away at you even if you handle it very well. And usually with a true invalidator, you have to handle it, and handle it, and handle it . . . ad nauseam, ad infinitum. Then if you do leave, the person who is a ranting, raving invalidator may suddenly get very soft, and may even admit to invalidating. He will do anything to get you back under his wing. He will tell you how miserable he is without you.

Then when you feel sorry for him and decide to come back, he will secretly consider you a fool for being sympathetic. He will wait for a time, then he will begin working to get you down again.

A true invalidator will say anything to keep you with him, because he has to *have* you, not because he loves you. Because he has to control you, not because he loves you. Because you fulfill his desires for power, not because he wants you. Because you serve *his* purpose, not because he is interested in you. He is interested in you only so that he can find your weaknesses and play on them, to control you.

It doesn't matter whether an invalidator is conscious or unconscious of what he does. He is still responsible for it. It doesn't matter if someone shoots you consciously or unconsciously . . . you still die. In the case of invalidation, it's sometimes harder to deal with someone who is unconscious of doing it. When confronted with what he is doing, he may say, "Where did you get that silly idea? You are invalidating me by accusing me of invalidation!" After he says that, you will probably be ready to tear him apart. However, there are some things to consider. First of all, if he is *unconsciously* invalidating you, there's a good chance he has been connected to an invalidator (mother, father, boss, spouse). When he gets angry at you, it may come out as invalidation. Being an "unconscious invalidator" is very hard for any person to confront. No one wants to think of him- or herself that way. Then again, it's not your problem that he doesn't recognize his problem. You must treat him "as if" he is conscious of it. In my opinion, the best you can do is (1) point it out, (2) stand your ground, or (3) disconnect if he is not willing to see it. He may come around only after he is faced with losing his relationship with you.

INTRODUCING THE VICTIM

People are born willing to listen, but after many years of being put down, a person may stop being willing to listen. People are also born willing to be wrong. But after an invalidator points out constantly what we do wrong, we may stop being willing to be wrong about anything.

Invalidators abuse willingness to listen by making so many critical or cutting remarks that the victim closes up and stops listening completely, to escape the terrible feeling of always appearing to be wrong. This defense allows the victim to stop hearing the invalidator and stops some of the pain of invalidation, but the reaction to the invalidator may also cause a person not to listen to anyone else, either. An invalidator's victim may try to appear totally righteous. The victim has lost the willingness to listen and the willingness to be wrong.

You may know someone who doesn't listen much and talks a lot. Was there an invalidator in his or her past?

Another person who has been injured by an invalidator may be very quiet and shy. He is afraid to open his mouth out of fear of being invalidated. He may seem to reject friendship with anyone, but that may spring from his fear. A shy person may be naturally quiet and reserved, or he may have been connected to an invalidator who stepped on his self-esteem whenever he spoke up for himself. There is a difference between choosing to be quiet and feeling stifled.

Still another product of an invalidator is someone

who is very stubborn. He may call himself "strong-willed." He has had it with invalidators, has decided to stand his ground no matter what, and will not change his mind under any circumstances. He is *never* wrong.

How can we correct our own behavior if we can't listen to others and if we can't afford to be wrong? The ruination of our God-given gift of communication is one of the most destructive things that one person can do to another. Equally devastating is the part we ourselves play when we allow someone else to force us to limit or distort our communication ability because of our fear of invalidation.

Most people are familiar with what might happen when Joe hurts Fred. Fred then may be motivated to hurt Joe. It's very simple. Someone does something to hurt you, and then you might want to do something to hurt him back.

However, what most people are not aware of is the following sequence of events:

1. Joe hurts Fred (i.e., Joe invalidates Fred).
2. Fred is unaware that Joe hurt him, but nevertheless he feels bad.
3. Joe sees that Fred feels bad and also sees that Fred is not going to return the hurt.
4. Joe, in order to be righteous about his actions, begins to invent "reasonable" excuses why he hurt Fred. He looks for motivations for having hurt Fred. Joe may say to himself, "Well, anyone who would let me walk all over him deserves to be hurt," or he could say, "That's just the way those fill-in-the-blank people are, so they deserve to be stepped on."
5. Once Joe has justified hurting Fred, he will continue to hurt Fred on the basis of his trumped-up motivations.
6. *Joe loses respect for Fred* because Fred allows himself to be hurt.

This may continue until Fred is mentally collapsed and has a nervous breakdown or worse, or until Fred finally confronts Joe and says something like, "Look, damn it! I'm not taking your @#* anymore!"

If Fred feels unworthy or inferior as a person, he may allow Joe to run him right into the ground. You may know someone, someone you consider to be a good person, who puts up with another who makes her life miserable. You wonder why she takes it. Possibly she feels unworthy of having someone nice to be with. She can't accept people being nice to her. She is attracted to people who put her down.

She has been able to handle invalidation—after all, she is *surviving*, isn't she? But if she should happen to get some praise or affection, she doesn't know how to deal with it.

The person who invalidates is not always the SOB. A passive-aggressive victim can create a scene in which it looks like he is being invalidated. Fred could set himself up to be invalidated by being sickeningly sweet and cowering around Joe. Did you ever meet someone you had the impulse to put down? This person might have the appearance of being the sweetest person in town, yet frequently makes unconscious, "little mistakes" without taking responsibility for them. This person might be late all the time and always have a good excuse for being late, and cower and make you look like a @#* for being upset with him. He is always putting himself down. The context of his interaction is "look how disgusting I am."

You tend to have no respect for someone who has no self-respect. When you congratulate him on something, he makes little of your congratulations because he can't *have* good will for himself. He may be a terrific person, and yet he will draw invalidators like a magnet. He will choose to have a lousy time with somebody you consider to be an SOB rather than a good time with you. If he is with you, he may constantly try to prove to you what a miserable, helpless loser he is. He has to be "right" in thinking that he is a victim, a lowly soul. He will set it up so the world proves this to him and to others constantly.

There is an invalidator in his past ... and *now* there is an invalidator inside his head. He's internalized the invalidator and turned it against himself. But look out—his misery loves company.

An invalidator sets up a context that says, *"You're wrong. You're wrong."* And a victim sees himself as a victim and will not own responsibility, and he works hard to prove he really is a victim so he can be "right" about it.

The victim will bend your ear constantly about the tragedies of his life. Horrible circumstances, drunken spouse, fire-destroyed house, unemployment—and someone else is always to blame. "They" did it to him again. He will explain it in such a way that he could do nothing about it. *"The car* drove off the highway and hit a tree." (He just happened to be sitting there drunk behind the steering wheel.) Then they took away his license, so he lost his job. And they fired him after six months of faithful service just because he couldn't come to work. He is very interested in having you agree with him so he can feel more justified in being a victim.

This person may not appreciate anything you do for him because he feels unworthy of it. You will seldom be able to please him or make him happy. Happiness is impossible for him. These people are perfect mates for invalidators. They survive on being miserable. If things go too well for them, they will create an upset in their lives.

You may find that your efforts to help this victim never seem to work. He always seems to mess up his life again—always unconsciously. You end up feeling impotent. And until this person recognizes his victim act and begins to do something about it, there isn't much you can do. He has to *intend* to change. He has to stop blaming his bad luck and his weak willpower for his problems, and decide to stop being a loser.

A person's integrity is based on his or her intentions. If a person intends to be valuable and intends to be worthy, then there is no stopping her. She will give up proving how unworthy she is. *Each person's worth is determined by that person alone.* If she *knows* she has good intentions, then she may encounter barriers to her self-realization, she may make mistakes on the way, but there is no proving that she is a rotten person or a miserable loser. There is no way to make her a victim, once she has decided not to be one anymore. Her life can be focused on developing her magnificence, and not on the mistakes or barriers that temporarily get in her way. She *intends* to free herself, and her *intention* frees her.

TWO DANCERS: AN EXAMPLE

Let's compare two dancers, looking at the way each one handles a setback in his practice.

The first dancer intends to do step X. Fails. Intends to do step X. Fails. Intends to do step X. Succeeds.

This dancer has focused his attention on the magnificence of his dancing. He pays attention to what he intends to do, and he knows how to get off the mistakes.

The second dancer wants to do step X. Fails. Complains about the slippery floor. Decides he will never get it right. Compares his dancing with that of the first dancer and feels inferior. Wants to do step X. Fails. Gets depressed. Dwells on what a rotten dancer he is. Blames parents for not sending him to ballet school when he was younger. Blames world for being so unfair that he was raised in a family with no money. Wants really *badly* to do step X. Finally, he either gives up or does step X at last.

If he finally succeeds in doing step X, he may then

compare himself to a lesser dancer who can't even do step X yet, and demonstrate his incredible ego.

Meanwhile, the first dancer has gone on to do steps Y and Z.

This chapter is not about two types of persons. If what you thought you got from this chapter is the ability to run around pinning labels of "victim" or "invalidator" on real people, then you didn't get much from this chapter. This chapter is describing and identifying phenomena that may partially or wholly exist in an individual. If you use the data in this book to make someone wrong . . . then this book is about *you*.

Pointing out invalidation to another for the purpose of *handling* it is not invalidating that person (although he or she may feel invalidated). Pointing out invalidation to another for the purpose of making him or her wrong *is* invalidating. It's the intention behind the words and actions that makes all the difference. In handling invalidation, you can get great confidence from knowing your intentions.

Nearly everyone has some of the traits of an invalidator. The one-percenter does it consciously, consistently, for personal gain, for power, for control, and without conscience. But everyone falls into the role of invalidator sometimes. Do YOU invalidate? Probably! You may do it when you feel someone has wronged you. You may do it as a defense. You may do it unconsciously. The next section of this book is addressed to the invalidator. It may help you recognize what someone is doing to you. But it also may help you recognize when *you* are the invalidator.

"Every time you meet a situation, though you think at the time it is an impossibility and you go through the tortures of the damned, once you have met it and lived through it, you find that forever after you are freer than you were before."

—Eleanor Roosevelt

3
The Cycle of Invalidation

TO AN INVALIDATOR

So. You have decided you are an invalidator. Or else you are not quite sure you are an invalidator. Or else you don't consider yourself to be an invalidator, but you are reading this section to see what the author will have to say to "them." If you admit to being an invalidator, you have my respect and acknowledgment for your willingness to confront this part of yourself.

We all react to things. Some hurt others. Some hurt themselves. The secret behind changing it is your *intention* and *willingness to know*. That's about it. It may sound simple. Actually, it is sometimes simple and sometimes very hard. Thank you for being willing to read this. Now that you've read more than half of my book and I've described the invalidator in great detail, I want you to know that I know . . . there is no such thing as an invalidator. That's right. There are only people and the mechanism of invalidation. It was my approach to use the term *invalidator*. If you thought you were . . . ta da! . . . an invalidator, that just shows how willing you are to put yourself down.

If you find yourself invalidating, work on that mechanism. Get out of that destructive role you ol' invalidator, you!

Maybe you think this doesn't really tell you how to stop invalidating. You want to stop *right now*. Well, tough. Your impatience is showing. If you read this chapter and understand it, then you will have the ability to clear it up for yourself. It will take time. I forgot to mention: another trait of an "invalidator" is . . . impatience.

WHY YOU ARE AN INVALIDATOR

Was there someone in your life who invalidated you? It could have been someone you loved or someone you hated. Invalidation is a mechanism that gets passed on from one to another. Who in your life was always "right"? Under whose thumb were you? Of whom were you afraid? These questions may assist you in locating a possible invalidator in your life. Who invalidated you, or who did you see invalidate others?

If you feel bad about yourself for invalidating, then chances are feeling bad about yourself will cause you to invalidate even more. Chances are good that you invalidate yourself more than anyone. You may feel like such an SOB, you may be so down on yourself, that you think someone who would love you must be even *worse* than you are, and therefore *deserving* to be invalidated. After all, anyone who would hang around with such a creep as you are must be really screwed up. Right?

HOW DO YOU STOP?

So, what should you do if you catch yourself invalidating and decide you'd like to stop doing it? Well, hang on to your hat and get ready to confront some things about yourself.

Maybe at some point in your life, someone made you so

wrong that you succumbed to being wrong, and you agreed that you were wrong. After that, you considered yourself to be basically wrong, or basically screwed up. You may also have made the assumption that others are basically nasty, too.

You may have spent a lot of your life *proving* that you were not messed up because you don't want to *appear* bad. So you feel as if you have to be righteous about yourself. You have to be right all the time. Well, now, how did all this come about?

It happened through the mechanism of invalidation, which gets passed from one person to another and one generation to another by contagion. Look at the chart on the following pages. Examine it first, and then come back here for clarification.

Let me try to explain in words what the chart is saying. Again, there is really no such thing as "an invalidator." There is a *person*, and then, besides the person, there is the *mechanism* of invalidation. A person may use this mechanism, but the *mechanism* is not the *person*. You may sometimes be attached to invalidation so closely you cannot see it. Sometimes you may feel the effect of invalidating. You may know you are doing it and you don't want to, and you don't like yourself for doing it to people, and still you just keep on doing it. It can be so frustrating that you finally just give up and accept yourself as an SOB. You define yourself as "bad" and you dramatize invalidation. You constantly find yourself invalidating, just as you yourself were invalidated. You feel *compelled* to do it. It seems to happen automatically sometimes, *because you identified with the invalidator*.

You think you have only two choices:

1. Be like the invalidator and SURVIVE.
2. Be like the invalidated and succumb.

You may come to believe that you must hurt or be hurt, control or be controlled. After all, in your past experience, the invalidator won and you lost. You *re-act*. Get it? You repeat the whole drama, but this time you try to be the winner, the SOB who can't be defeated.

You may *re-act* in certain situations, almost like a machine. That's not you out there; that's just your dramatization of negative experiences you had years ago. When you are re-acting, or invalidating someone automatically because it was once done to you, who really gets invalidated?

If there ever was a Satan, he wouldn't have wanted to work very hard to pollute souls. He probably would have resorted to inventing a set of nasty archetypes that would spread from one person to another by contagion. After all, if he was so evil, he wouldn't want to struggle. It would be easier to throw a couple of turds into still water and watch it ripple. So he invented invalidation! And he made it contagious. We did the rest.

Maybe sometimes you are not into invalidation and sometimes you are. It may almost seem that you are two different people, one who has good intentions and is very supportive, and one who sometimes takes over, making you into an "invalidation entity." This evil entity is not you, but a role you are playing: the role of invalidator.

You probably feel a sense of unreality when you are in that role. You act very controlling, but you may feel that you are being controlled. You may appear to others to be very demanding and authoritative. But inside you feel very helpless and scared. That demanding, authoritarian, invalidating entity is your act, which you re-act, re-act, and re-act.

WHAT HAPPENS TO INVALIDATORS?

Two things happen to invalidators. Some of them see that invalidation doesn't work in the long run. This can happen through life hints. If a person gets enough of these hints and is paying attention, his or her behavior changes.

But not everyone gets the hint, and then what happens is rather sad. There is a natural cycle that people go through when they hurt others:

1. Hurt someone.
2. Admit wrongdoing, at least to oneself.
3. Feel guilt—not neurotic guilt, but real guilt.
4. Atone—do something to make up for it.

The invalidator's problem is that he can't admit being wrong, so he doesn't go through the natural cycle. He has more of a deny-and-suppress pattern.

1. Hurt someone.
2. Justify hurting that person, to oneself.
3. Suppress guilt which eventually turns into a "bad mood."
4. Avoid atonement.

THE MECHANISM OF INVALIDATION

Person A = The Invalidator   Person B = The Invalidated

Characteristics of Person A

Feels inadequate
Feels angry
Feels compelled to control
Unwilling to listen
Unwilling to be wrong
Unwilling to introvert, to
   look at own motives

Characteristics of Person B

At First:

Willing to listen
Willing to be wrong
Willing to introvert, to look at
   own motives

After Association with A:
Unexpressed anger
Feeling of being wrong
Feeling of inability to control

After Prolonged Association:
Defines self as bad, wrong
To protect self, becomes:
   Unwilling to listen
   Unwilling to be wrong
   Unwilling to introvert, to
     look at own motives

Finally, to survive:
Identifies with invalidator.
Does what the invalidator
   does—invalidator has control
Invalidator appears right.
Invalidator won.

SO THE CYCLE BEGINS AGAIN

Person B has been transformed from the *victim* of Person A to the *invalidator* of Person C. Person B is now re-acting in the archetype of invalidator. Invalidation is *contagious.*

Person B = The Invalidator   Person C = The Invalidated

Characteristics of Person B

Feels inadequate
Feels angry (finally surfaces,
   but directed at innocent
   bystander)
Feels compelled to control
   (out of fear of being
   controlled again)
Unwilling to listen
Unwilling to be wrong
Unwilling to introvert, to
   look at own motives

Characteristics of Person C

Willing to listen
Willing to be wrong
Willing to introvert, to look at
   own motives

The suppressed guilt stays inside and gathers until the invalidator begins to feel depressed. Or he may become psychosomatically ill.

Maybe you've met a person who behaves this way. The demonic personality is a kind of manic state. The person seems to have no conscience; he seems to enjoy manipulation and putting other people down.

In this phase, the invalidator is carefree. He doesn't notice and doesn't care about the feelings of others. He goes right on doing selfish things like drinking, playing around on his wife, or belittling others until, unexpectedly, he suddenly falls apart.

Now he enters an exaggerated state of remorse, or gets very sick, as his relationships with everyone start to fall apart. He gets sick, especially if his spouse leaves him, so the spouse feels obligated to come back and take care of him. The illness punishes him *and* gets the spouse back at the same time.

Beware of the invalidator who doesn't get sick and does not have remorse. This one is bad news. His cycle is different. He doesn't *really* care about anyone but himself. He is extremely selfish. He is conscious of his invalidating and probably even works at perfecting it. This is the Hitler. This is the one-percenter. (Previously in this chapter we've been talking about the twenty-percenters. The twenty-percenters have enough conscience left to feel remorse at least.)

You've watched this one-percenter destroy people. The people around him are afraid of him, but in his control. He is not a total devil; *no one* is. Most of the time he leads what looks like a normal life. It's just that he is *so* selfish and possessive. And, every once in a while, he does something that will make a lasting scar on someone close to him. By the time he is done living his lifetime, the world is worse for his having been there.

You may have seen a person like this in action. He is

selfish. He has no conscience. He is controlling of others and manipulative. He has no sympathy and no mercy. You may have watched him drive someone crazy or lead someone to commit suicide. You wonder how he gets away with it. You wonder why he lives that way. You wonder what will ever happen to him. I think I can tell you that. I've watched a person like this lead his life.

I watched helplessly while an invalidator ruthlessly invalidated his wife to suicide. It was a nonstop, merciless deed. He showed no conscience even though he had been with her for forty years. Of course, she was into a victim act and eventually made herself so weak she couldn't stand up to him anymore. She died on the day she committed suicide. He had been dead long before that.

The tools of invalidation arc available for you to use right now. You or anyone can pick them up, practice them, and perfect them with repetition. But if you think invalidating people is a good way of controlling others, think twice.

Let's suppose you made use of a demonic archetype in which you were selfish and manipulative. Eventually you would really hurt someone, and then a natural remorse would tap you on the shoulder to remind you of your misdeeds. You might drop the selfish behavior and atone, get depressed, or get sick.

You use these mechanisms on a "buy now, pay later" plan. Sure, you can run around feeling carefree, not caring about others, for a while. But sooner or later you are going to end up alone and lonely. People eventually catch on, no matter how gregarious and fun-loving you are. Once people realize that you are completely taken up with yourself, they get turned off. Besides, there seems to be a natural law that eventually leads to the destruction of a person like this. After all, how can a person remain a human being and constantly destroy his or her own foundations as a human being?

If you repress remorse, you repress *all* feelings to that same degree. You also give up part of your ability to gauge how other people feel. So each time you repress *real* remorse, you die a little. You cannot lose touch with your own conscience without losing touch with others, because your conscience is the bridge that connects you to others.

The worst thing that can happen is that you become so selfish that you mess up all your relationships. You lose contact so badly that you can't understand other people at all. You lose your own feelings so that you can no longer experience love, beauty, friendship, or any of the meaningful experiences in life. You have to resort to booze, drugs, or degraded sex to feel anything at all. It's only the fleeting sensations, the "wow" moments, that are fun. You avoid anything meaningful.

You don't have to take my word for all this. I am sure you have met people who are so far gone into themselves that they have lost their ability to understand others They constantly invalidate others. They are also prone to moodiness or depression because nobody can stay in that totally selfish pattern forever.

If you think you can ever be happy living that way, think again. Watch for invalidation so you can handle it.

Know exactly what it is. Know it and see it and sidestep it. Make invalidation lose its effect.

When someone tells you of something you did wrong, take a look at her intention in telling you that. Even if what she says is absolutely true, even if you did exactly what she is saying you did, look at her *intention*. Is she invalidating you, or is she trying to wise you up for your own sake?

And look at your *own* intentions. When you criticize someone, or point out a mistake or a misdeed, are you doing it for that person's own good or to hurt?

When you are angry, do you get angry at innocent bystanders? Do you have to get mad at someone? Can you get angry freely at inanimate objects, or just get angry, period? If you need a whipping boy, clean up your act. Anger *should* be expressed. But not at an innocent person.

When you detect an invalidator, whether it's someone near you or you yourself, show a little compassion. This poor unfortunate soul is either in hell or on his way. And what is more, never label *anyone* an invalidator. People are people. What people do is what people do. Attacking a person instead of attacking what that person is doing just doesn't work in the long run. You're just letting invalidation breed invalidation.

TO THE INVALIDATED WHO *DOESN'T* INVALIDATE

Well, now, you are the "victim" of invalidation, but you don't invalidate. Ah yes. You are not like those others. You *never* put anyone down. You *never* get angry. You were connected to an invalidator at one time, and you see it all now. So, now you're reading about them with a big halo glimmering about two inches above your head.

You don't know how to get angry without hurting

people, so you hold it all inside. You were made so wrong at one point that you made a forced decision that you were completely OK. That's where you got your halo. Along with that decision, you developed an unwillingness to be wrong. But you made out better than some people; you didn't lose your willingness to listen.

Now you do the flip side of the work of an invalidator. You *listen* to people. You make people *right*. You never get angry. You've been invalidated by someone, and you certainly don't want to hurt people the way that person did. So you become dishonest with your true feelings. You fool people to build their egos.

So, now you believe you are perfectly OK. You are afraid to look at anything that doesn't agree with that premise. Being something of a pompous ass by now, you won't look at ways you could change, because that would be admitting there is something wrong with you. To you, this idea is very frightening. Instead of seeing a change in your thinking as self-improvement, you feel ashamed of it, as a sign that something is wrong with you. However, the paradox is that to be perfect, you have to be willing to look at your imperfections. It is especially difficult for someone who has been made wrong to be willing to appear wrong. Your willingness to be wrong has been abused. You may now have a big scar there, and you may feel completely vulnerable.

If you have made a defensive decision that you are perfectly OK, you might desperately try to hold on to this state. You might become terribly opposed to change. You were once in a situation where deciding you were OK meant your ego *survival*. So you will go to great lengths to maintain this belief. If you are approached with a mistake you are making, or if someone sees you are in trouble and tries to help, you may react with fear. If you find yourself changing your opinions or your point of view, you may become terrified and feel you are finally succumbing as you almost did to the invalidator long ago. You may quickly escape from any change and fall back on your old beliefs. You are willing to look at new ideas only if they do not threaten your basic determination that you are OK right now, just as you are, and you always have been perfectly OK. You may be perceived by others as a weird person, because your mind becomes a mishmash of modern ideas and antiquated attitudes. You may develop a lot of funny quirks in your personality, because nothing can be allowed to shake the foundations of the basic structure you are holding on to.

A healthy person realizes that he is OK, and he can accept other people's opinions and judgments. He is willing to see that sometimes someone else can be right and he can be wrong, and that helps keep his feelings in balance. But if a person has been *forced* to define himself as perfectly OK, in order to defend himself against someone who wanted to invalidate him, he may not be able to accept opinions other than his own. It was the judgments of another person that pushed him to this defensive position in the first place, so now he feels he can *never* be wrong, especially if his mistake is pointed out by another person.

A likable personality—one that never gets angry and always builds egos—is the flip side of the invalidator personality. But this character type has its problems, too. The invalidator sprays anger all over, and this causes problems for her victims and for herself. But the victim who cannot and will not express *any anger at all* represses his anger, and probably has to repress most of his other feelings along with it. Both feel righteous. Both feel inadequate. The only way out of this trap is to be able to listen, to be able to express anger constructively, to be able to be wrong and to change when the situation requires it. And if everyone could live that way—there would be *no invalidators!*

"Only the weak are cruel. Gentleness can only be expected from the strong."

—Leo Buscaglia

4
What Do We Do About It?

INVALIDATOR BOSS?

What do you do if your boss invalidates constantly?
Let's be practical about this.

You could decide he or she is just an SOB. You could
set out to get him or her for all the misery you've
endured. This wouldn't say much for your integrity, and
you'd have to live with yourself, knowing that your
intentions were vengeful. It would also justify your
boss's outlook on life. Your boss might expect this of
people. Besides, it wouldn't work.

You could tell him off. This would allow you to
release your pent-up emotion, but it wouldn't work. He
might invalidate you more than ever, and you might not
keep your job let alone get a raise.

You probably won't be able to reason with your boss
while he is in his demon personality. It's better to wait
until he is himself. If the demon is all there is to your
boss, then I suggest you start looking for a new job
right now. He may be too far gone to help or to deal
with at all.

One thing you know: If he is invalidating you, he
must have learned it from somebody, possibly a domi-

neering mother or a controlling father. It may not have been either of his parents, but maybe *his* boss. Maybe he thinks that's the way a boss is supposed to act. It has happened that, if the president of the company is a habitual invalidator, everyone down the line takes on that behavior. After all, it is contagious.

More than anything else, an invalidator has to be right. Never, never say "you're wrong" to an invalidator; this is a cardinal rule. If you contradict, point out, demonstrate, or in any way show an invalidator to be wrong, sooner or later he will *get* you. Sooner or later you will pay. Invalidators are extremely revengeful. To an invalidator, being wrong is the most horrible thing that can happen to him, and he will *not* thank the person who puts him in that position. The best thing to do is acknowledge an invalidator; this does *not* mean to agree.

Example: An invalidator shares his opinion with you about the other employees. She says, "You know, those people out there are all for themselves. Nobody cares about this department." The worst thing you can say is, "No, you're wrong. Those people are dedicated and concerned people." The best thing you can do is to acknowledge what she says and try to see if there is some reason she said it. You might say, "You think so?" in such a vague way as to acknowledge what she said and allow her to talk more about it. There may be something specific that made her think that way. Perhaps she just walked by someone who took an extra two minutes at break time. Later, when she isn't being critical and doesn't suspect that you are trying to prove her wrong, you can point out some unselfish things the employees have done.

One thing that invalidators respond to best is affinity. If you like her, she may even allow you to prove her wrong, once in a while. That goes for almost anyone, of course. If you like someone and show that person a great deal of affinity, you can say practically anything to him or her. Be sure you always do it in private. An invalidator takes "being wrong" in front of a group as a terrible humiliation.

If you show that you *like* your boss, you will gain benefits beyond reason. Invalidators are excellent at logic, so they don't put much stock in it. But affinity is something they lack, and they can use a lot of it. After all, someone in this person's past probably chewed him up with logic, and pushed him away at the same time.

It also helps if you can find a genuine reason to look up to your boss. Invalidators are usually me-me-me people. Their self-esteem is actually low, but they hide this well by displaying overinflated egos. An invalidator may *think* of himself as the only important person around, but he may *feel* inferior to others. He uses his self-importance to try to make up for the inferiority. It's a confusing paradox—but ignore it at your peril.

With this knowledge, you can realize that the apparently strong, confident, ruthless boss might actually feel inside like a scared little kid. He may be someone to be pitied, not someone to be feared.

It's ironic but the best way to make an invalidator lose his grip is to invalidate him. A person who is trying to hurt another will use the methods that would hurt *him*. If you want to hurt an invalidator, all you need to do is watch what he does or says to others. If you use his own methods against him, he will cave in sooner than anyone. It's so obvious it's almost funny.

However, if you choose this method, you should realize that you may be putting your job on the line. This may actually be the most positive career step you can make, though it can be a hard one. You may want to line up another job before you try it. Invalidating your boss may give you a feeling of satisfaction as you stand in the unemployment line.

If your boss embarrasses you in front of a group, and

you want to get him back, embarrass *him* in front of a
group. But be careful. He has probably been embarrassing people in groups for years, and he is probably much
better at it than you are. But you'll have the benefit of
surprise, so his endurance won't be as good.

INVALIDATOR SPOUSE?

It is typical for one partner to be dominant. Someone
has to have the final say, or marriages wouldn't work. It
is probably best if the responsibilities are divided up in
such a way that each gets to have the final say about half
the time. That way, each one is the boss sometimes. That
makes for a happy relationship.

But how many marriages do you know of that are
happy? The relationship of husband/wife has more
invalidation in it than any other. It is a worldwide
disease. It seems as if the usual pattern is to get married,
eventually do irreversible harm to the relationship, and
then regret getting married.

One of the problems of our society is that we can't
seem to rehabilitate a marriage once it has gone bad. We
wait until things are intolerable before we seek help.
Then we don't really want help, we want out. It is
similar to people who did drugs in the sixties. Some
caused permanent damage to themselves. They now say,
"If only I had known, back then."

Just because someone seems to be controlling the
family doesn't mean he or she is necessarily an invalidator. His or her mate could simply be irresponsible;
someone has to manage things.

There are lots of "nice" ways to invalidate, too. Like
the silent treatment, when you don't acknowledge what
your spouse said. Or telling your legitimately irate
spouse that she looks "cute" when she's angry.

A person using invalidation could be perfectly unconscious of doing so. The victim could also be uncon-

scious of it. Whether the invalidator and victim (or two invalidators!) are conscious or unconscious of their patterns, two people who initially love each other can get caught up in this scenario, and it degrades the whole family over time. The person doing most of the invalidating is not made aware of it until it is too late: the love has died and the damage is irreparable.

Have you ever met someone who was surprised when his or her spouse left? Things were so wonderful, and then BANG . . . she or he runs off with a circus performer! It could have been unconscious invalidation at work.

Even if the invalidator is made aware, he may not be made properly aware. He may just suppress his invalidating tendencies instead of correcting them. He may hold back his feelings instead of learning how to let them out constructively. Sooner or later, the old behavior unleashes itself, and he loses relationship after relationship.

Many times, the invalidator is not motivated to change, because he is the "winner." He has these powerful mechanisms backing him up, so he doesn't suffer in the short run. Often, however, he damages the marriage permanently before he is aware of it.

While it is true that some people are irreversible invalidators, there aren't that many of them. It's worth making the effort to break the negative pattern of invalidation. If the invalidator finds that invalidation no longer works, he or she might be motivated to change. If you are being invalidated, it's "your" problem. Once you no longer allow the invalidator to control you, he will finally have to deal with himself; his problems remain his.

Try the following:

1. Identify the problem for the invalidator.
2. Set limits for behavior of the invalidator—what is and is not acceptable to you.

3. Set a time limit for change.
4. Pay attention to what the invalidator *does* rather than what he or she says.

If invalidation is a way of life for your spouse, you may have no alternative except to separate. However, I have found that in many cases, the marriage *is* fixable. Also, be sure that you are not leaving just to invalidate your spouse!

ONE SEQUENCE FOR HANDLING INVALIDATION

If we wanted to, we could fit all ways of handling things into two categories:

1. Reason (e.g., parent to child, "Don't go out into the street, dear, because you may get hit by a car.")
2. Cause-effect (e.g., parent to child, "YOU WENT OUT INTO THE STREET AGAIN!!!" (Smack!!)

People who have great reasoning capabilities sometimes have a great deal of trouble understanding cause-effect solutions. Their world is very logical, and they may have had great success solving situations that way. They tend to believe that almost anything can be handled with reason and logic. They tend to be philosophical about life and try to be very fair about everything. And perhaps they are a little afraid of things that are irrational or beyond comprehension. (These are the people who were incapable of believing that Hitler was herding Jews into gas furnaces by the millions.) These people are easy to invalidate because they naively believe in the good intent of everyone. They think it was a joke or slip of the tongue if someone cuts into them.

Then there are people who do not put much stock in logic, reason, or philosophy. These people have been manipulated by it, lied to, and deceived by it. They have learned to pay more attention to what people *do* rather than to what they *say*. These are the ones who fire you because you called in sick too much . . . no matter what the reason. They may appear to be listening to you, but actually they will be looking at your expressions and actions, trying to size you up by your appearance rather than your thought processes.

Mr. Reason and Mr. Cause-Effect do not have a very good understanding of one another when they are in their purest form, because they are at opposite ends of a continuum:

Reason   Cause-Effect

←————————————————————————→

Thank goodness most of us are somewhere in between. There is no right or wrong about it. Perhaps "balance" would be "right."

There 's no set of rules to handle invalidation that work every time, but let's take a look at a sequence that has had some success.

First try reason.

Handle the invalidator with . . .

- Humor
- Respect
- Affinity
- Professionalism
- Acknowledgment
- Diplomacy
- Patience
- With discretion
- Firmness
- Specific, impersonal, but personable comments
- Words that tell how you feel

Don't . . .

- Generalize
- Label
- Judge
- Blame
- Make him or her wrong
- Be righteous
- Make it personal
- Insinuate
- Act out your angry feelings, or
- Make him or her feel guilty

If reasoning doesn't work, try cause-effect:

- Hurt him when he invalidates.
- Invalidate him. (Show him how it feels.)
- Do something outrageous. (Talk loudly. Act crazy. Squirt him with a water gun. Pee on his flowers. Laugh shrilly as if he just told you a joke. Wink at him. Make flatulent noises.)
- Insult him.
- Squeeze his cheek.
- Raise your eyebrows at him.
- Stare at him unwaveringly.
- Disconnect/quit/leave.

The cause-effect reactions you give to the invalidator make him uncomfortable whenever he invalidates. I had a psychology professor whom a bunch of us tried to manipulate using behavioral techniques. He used to pace back and forth across the room, and it was annoying to us. So every time he walked over to the right, we would yawn or act bored. When he walked to the left, we would act attentive. By the end of the semester, he was sitting on a stool to the far left of the room without ever knowing our little plot!

If your invalidator actually likes any of the above cause-effect reactions and enters into a game with you, stop doing what you are doing and move on to the next step in your cause-effect plan. If you run out of steps, I am sure you will think of something. Get the idea?

Drug dealers keep selling drugs because they go to court and nothing happens. If the drug dealer is a cause-effect person, he will say the right things, or get the right lawyer and get out on probation. In his mentality, nothing happened! In some cases, one good punch in the nose would give the dealer enough of a "reality adjustment" that he would say to himself, "Ouch! That hurt! No more selling drugs for me!"

Again, I must remind you. If you know the mechanisms, you can find a way to deal with invalidation that fits *your* personality and *your* ethics. No book can cover every situation. You won't be a pro from reading this book, just as you won't be a pro from reading a guidebook to baseball. All you get are the rules.

Since people ask me for some specific things that they can try, I am going to give you some approaches that seem to work most of the time and some examples of what I have seen others do to confront invalidation. Please remember, however, to do it your way

CONFRONTING

What a great word *confronting* is! You just look at the person who invalidated you in such a way that you show you know exactly what she is doing. A long pause or a knowing smile, resting your chin in your hand, or leaning forward slightly can let her know she had better not mess with you.

Example: Father-in-law has been asking (interrogating) son-in-law about his job all evening at dinner, looking for buttons to push. Finally, father-in-law gets red in the face, turns on fire eyes and booming voice and says, "What kind of a job is that for a man to have?" Son-in-law says nothing, but keeps looking at father-in-law calmly. Father-in-law raises voice, increases the red color, and opens eyes wider while ranting and raving. Son-in-law still just looks at him calmly. Finally father-in-law looks away, rants and raves to the other people at the table, lowers voice, gets up from the table and leaves.

Son-in-law did not "get into it." He did not cower. He did not agree or give in. He maintained contact with the father-in-law. The father-in-law felt uncomfortable enough to leave and won't be inclined to do it again.

REPEAT THAT PLEASE

Asking the person to repeat the invalidation will many times water it down, especially if it was an insinuation or something that he was trying to sneak by you. If he is brave enough to repeat it again arrogantly, you can say, "Oh. That's what I *thought* you said." Usually, however, the little coward will not repeat it the way he said it the first time.

TELL THE WHOLE TRUTH

A lot of invalidations are double messages riddled with insinuations, voice inflections, tone, and other clues besides the actual words. All you need to do is to size up everything and tell the simple truth.

Example 1: A woman attends a professional meeting with her peer group, which is made up mostly of men. Frank says, "Susan, take the minutes of the meeting, would you, dear?" Caught off guard, Susan says, "I don't have a notepad." Frank says, "Come on, Susan! You came to this meeting without a note pad!? (sarcasm)."

Susan's reply: "Frank, you are talking as if it is my job to take the minutes of this meeting. I suggest you ask one of us to take the minutes *before* the meeting starts instead of waiting till the last minute and having to make these arrangements after the meeting starts."

Susan did not get defensive. She did not accuse Frank of asking her to take minutes just because she was a woman. She did not let him push her buttons (i.e., introvert her). She merely stated things that were factual and thereby made Frank's attitude obvious.

Example 2: At work Al is presenting the proposal for a project he is working on. Bill is sitting at the meeting looking more and more irritated. Bill's face is red. He is breathing loudly and exasperatedly. No one understands what Al is saying because they are caught up in wondering what is bothering Bill. Finally Al addresses Bill: "Bill, is there something you want to say?"

Bill stands up with the veins popping out of his temples, "I sure do want to say something! You don't know what the hell you are talking about. Why, I've never seen. . . ."

Al nails him with the truth. Al has to raise his voice to get above Bill's: "*Bill.* You came in here and were acting irritated even before I started my presentation. I don't see how you could make a judgment based only on what I have said so far. I want you to show me the respect to let me finish my presentation."

"Yeah?!" says Bill, "Well, you are not wasting my time."

Al's reply is the truth: "Bill, you are embarrassing me in front of all these people. I'd like them to make up their own minds about what I am going to say. You don't have to stay at the meeting. I can talk to you later if you like."

With that, Bill stomps out of the meeting saying, "I'm not interested in what *you* have to say."

Al says to the group, "Why don't we take a five-minute stretch break."

The break allows everyone to talk the scene out instead of think about it during Al's presentation.

You can always tell the truth by looking at your feelings:

- "I feel embarrassed."
- "I feel angry that you said it that way."
- "I feel put on the spot."

No one can argue with the way you feel, because (right or wrong) it *is* the way you feel.

GET THEM ALONE

People who embarrass you in front of a group use the group for their power. If you get them alone, you may find that they squirm in their seat and become apologetic. They learn to have respect for you because they know you will confront them instead of hiding behind a group. Reason with them first. If they embarrass you again, threaten to do the same to them. "How would you like it if I embarrassed you in front of everyone? Do it to me again, and I will have a little surprise for you."

The surprise is the truth: "Bill, there you go again trying to embarrass me in front of everyone. Can't you think of a more professional way to handle yourself?"

MIRROR THE PROJECTION

When someone accuses you of something you didn't do, check to see if he or she has done it. When someone threatens you with something, threaten that person back with the very same thing. (Chances are he or she is threatening you with what he or she is most afraid of.) When someone accuses you of not liking him or her or of being prejudiced, guess who doesn't like whom? Guess who is prejudiced? When someone tells you that you must choose A or B, tell the person you are not going to choose, and he or she can choose what to do about it.

Example 1: Dave says, "Look. It's either me or your career." Mary says, "I'm not choosing."

Example 2: Fred says, "I don't think you like me." You say, "Do *you* like *me*, Fred?"

Example 3: Martha says, "I think you have been taking money from the business for yourself." You say, "Have you taken any money that you haven't told me about?"

WHAT TO TELL CHILDREN WHEN THEY ASK WHY PEOPLE ARE NASTY OR MEAN

Usually, people are mean for one of three reasons:

1. To get their way
2. Because someone was nasty to them
3. Because they don't feel good about themselves

Sometimes someone who doesn't feel good about himself will think you are better than he is, so he tries to make you look small. Then he can feel better. The best thing to do is to show that person that you care about him and that he is OK. If you are mean to him, you'll just be "proving" that he is as bad as he thinks he is. But if you point out what you like about him, he may feel better—you have made him realize he has some good qualities. If he realizes he is OK too, he won't have to be nasty.

Sometimes it's hard to find something good about someone, so then you might say that person has nice eyes, or is strong. Sometimes you don't have to say anything. A pat on the back and a smile will help. It doesn't always work. Some people can be so mean that it is best to just stay away from them.

When people are mean to you, you must remember

that *you* are OK. Maybe they didn't like something you did, but you are OK. If they are mean for no reason, maybe they are just in a bad mood, or they have a miserable life. Don't feel bad about yourself. Try to look at them and see why they are mean. You may say, "I'm sorry you are upset. Can I do something for you?" Sometimes if you give someone a hug, that's all it takes.

But you must be careful that people do not take advantage of you. Don't be afraid to say no in a friendly way. Smile, but don't give in. You don't have to do whatever they ask. If you don't think it is right, tell them, "I can't do that."

A SUMMARY FOR COPING WITH INVALIDATION

Realize the "invalidator" is a personality—not a person.

Invalidators usually look big but feel small. Paradoxically, they have low self-esteem but large egos.

The invalidator invalidates when he or she feels inferior or out of control. The one-percenter invalidates whenever he or she feels it will give him or her control and power.

No matter how manipulative in appearance, the twenty-percenter invalidator is usually unconscious, or only semiconscious, of what he or she is doing.

It is very difficult, if not impossible, to deal with an invalidator while you are in a state of introversion. First extrovert—take a look at the situation. Next, try to determine what is going on. Your biggest cues are intention and feelings. Is it the invalidator's intention to hurt you or help you? Is this communication distorted? If the *intention* is not good and the *feelings* are not good, invalidation is probably taking place in one of its many forms.

Invalidation is contagious. If you have been invalidated, you are more likely to slip into doing it yourself.

If someone is invalidating you, he or she has probably been invalidated in the past.

At first, you slip easily in and out of the invalidator personality. But the more you use this mechanism, the more you depend on it. Finally, you seem to *become* the role—*the invalidator*. But remember, there is no such animal. There are only *people*, and the things that people do. Anyone can become an invalidator. And anyone can stop it.

Invalidation works in the short run, not in the long run. You can win a lot of battles but lose the war.

5
To Invalidation: The Mechanism

My research on invalidation was prompted by experiences I personally have had with the mechanism. I watched helplessly while I saw someone I cared about being invalidated literally to death. At first, I blamed the "invalidator," but then I realized that he, too, was a victim of invalidation. I wrote a statement about the process when I was overwhelmed; it was a rather intense moment in my life. But it contains my intentions. It's a statement to invalidation itself.

TO INVALIDATION

You are this tremendous burden that impinges on me, whether I like it or not. You take no responsibility but create more and more unwanted responsibility for me. You come from the bowels of the physical universe. You are destructive. You are evil. You kill people. You degrade people. You create egomaniacs from your evil power. You enable people to suppress via your control mechanisms. You are sneaky. You have no conscience. You abuse the cherished things in life and spoil them.

You create more evil with evil. You create sickness, and you *are* sickness. You are one of the sinister archetypes. You re-create yourself.

People have used destructive forces to destroy you. They have killed people, but not you. You have been used against yourself. Invalidators have been invalidated. This has perpetuated you with the illusion that you were defeated. In crusades, the victors have to use evil to conquer, and in so doing, the victors become evil themselves. You are paradoxical. You are subtle in your righteousness. You are a quirk.

But you shall be conquered. You shall be exposed to the world. And in your nakedness you shall be helpless. You shall carry no force. You shall be anticipated. I will persist. I am not merely a Don Quixote. I know how you work. I know your weaknesses. I am not being destructive. I will not persist against you. My approach will be to extract the *being* from the *mechanism*. You as a mechanism cannot operate except subtly, and I shall remove the subtlety and make you known. The being will see you, thereby separating himself from what you are. He will be who he is, and you will be just a mechanism. And the paradox is that no one will destroy you. They will just choose not to nourish you, and you will die.

I will do all this not out of ego—not for credit. I do it out of love for my self. My self as humanity. I do it out of choice. And I have chosen to be completely responsible for you.

I attempt to unmask you, not for the evil purpose of trying to destroy evil, but to free myself and others from this paradox. I can see, as a prophecy, that evil will diminish as a result.

I will carry my distaste for you. I will enjoy seeing you disappear. Your elimination will give me sustenance. And my purpose will be love, and not destruction. So this is the beginning of your end. When this secret is exposed, it will no longer be effective.

If you have read this far, I know you are a person who wants to improve yourself and improve the way people live around you and with you. I wanted to share "To Invalidation" with you so that together we can work a miracle for generations to come. Invalidation can be terrible for an individual, but the problem really stems from an "us" problem. I want all my great-great-grand-children and yours to live in happiness and harmony. If we don't do something about invalidation, who will? And if it's not now, then when? I think it has to be *us* and it has to be *now*.

Although I may not be able to answer all correspondence, I am interested in knowing how this book has affected your life. You may write me at:

P.O. Box 6048
Wyomissing, PA 19610

You may also use this address to contact me regarding speaking engagements or audio and video cassette workshops on the subject.

Bibliography

Berne, Eric. *Games People Play.* New York: Ballantine. 1978.

Bramson, Robert. *Coping with Difficult People.* New York: Anchor Press/Doubleday, 1981.

Carter, James. *Self Analysis: The Book About Life.* Oreland, PA: Crusader Press, 1983.

English, O. Spurgeon, M.D., and Gerald H. J. Pearson. M.D. *Emotional Problems of Living.* New York: Norton. 1963.

Griffin, George. *The Case of the Costly Neurotic,* unpublished paper. March 1983.

Hubbard, L. Ron. *Self Analysis.* Los Angeles, California: The American Saint Hill Organization, 1950.

Jung, C. G. *Man and His Symbols.* New York: Doubleday and Co., 1964.

Lombardo, Michael M., and Morgan W. McCall, Jr. *Coping with an Intolerable Boss.* North Carolina: Center for Creative Leadership, 1984.

Payne, Robert. *The Life and Death of Adolf Hitler.* New York: Praeger Publishers, 1973.

Prather, Hugh. *Notes on Love and Courage.* New York: Doubleday, 1977.

Sheridan, John H. *Executives at the Breaking Point,* unpublished paper. Cleveland, Ohio: 1979.